Emotional Archives

Crystal Mott

Emotional Archives © 2021 Crystal Mott

All rights reserved.

No part of this publication may be reproduced, stored in a retrieval system, or transmitted, in any form or by any means, electronic, mechanical, photocopying, recording or otherwise, without the prior written permission of the presenters.

Crystal Mott asserts the moral right to be identified as author of this work.

Presentation by *BookLeaf Publishing*

Web: www.bookleafpub.com

E-mail: info@bookleafpub.com

ISBN: 9789357445597

First edition 2021

DEDICATION

To my Love,

without him I would not have found my courage

I love you

Never say never

Never say never,

you don't know what could be around the corner,

what's waiting for you to accomplish,

the hardships and triumphs that you will go through.

If you say never, you are not open to new things

Just robbing yourself of your future,

Be brave little one, there's bigger things out there for you.

Emotional Bathing

She bathed in her emotions

Let them wash over her

For she will no longer hide

She was wrong, they were wrong

Her voice needed to be heard

Her words needed to be felt

So she began her journey to unlearn all that she had known

She will no longer hide

You will see her and she cannot be unseen.

Forever means forever

A lie I was once told

To be loved unconditionally

A lie that hurt my soul

To have my heart torn to pieces

Not woman enough, I was told

Taken all he could

Nothing left to give

Rock bottom was where I was found

Forever means forever

A lie I was once told

A lesson that I needed to learn

They don't have what you have

You are so different

Your the one, shes the one

Forever means forever

A lie I was once told

To be hurt beyond redemption

A lesson I must learn

So began the rebirth of I

Forever means forever

A lie I needed to be told.

Generously giving

As she lay there she realised

She always feels as if she has to fight

For a part in their lives.

But when she stops and looks

She sees who is fighting for their part.

She gives herself so generously

To everyone but herself.

When she finally realises who she is

Everything will fall into place

It has to.

Whose view

So many had different views of her

Which were true to her

Who was she?

She believed she was a bit of everyone views

She was hard and soft

Insightful and daft

Scared and brave

She was complicated.

Tortured Souls

The heart ache burning their potential

No one taught them to love

No desire to be different

Who will love someone

Not willing to love them.

Its expected to love someone

Your taught to find a mate

To be together always

But to not love your mate

A forever and always won't exist.

My Love

His beauty didn't come from his jaw line,

It didn't come from the curves of his torso,

She did not see the strength in his arms,

She seen the way his lips twitched just before his face lit up from his smile.

She adored his inner strength,

The way he loved through his war,

He wasn't letting anyone bring him down.

A man with such strength looked into her eyes deeply,

His voice soothed her inner storm,

He caressed her body with a gentleness she had never felt.

How he understood her more then those who spent everyday knowing her,

And for all this and more she was falling deeply.

The man who stood in front of her tearing down her walls,

As they crumbled down she felt safer then ever before,

In the arms of the man she adored.

For she felt like he was seeing her,

Not her pretty face, not her story, nor what she had to offer.

She felt seen!

What a remarkable man and so she called him,

My love.

Unconditional

The unspoken words between two souls

love unshared felt deep in her core

He had her love unconditionally

She felt loved, adored and cherished

Everyday she chose him to be a part of her world

He was so important to her

Did he know how much she loved him

Could she share herself whole heartedly.

Why did she doubt their connection

When she had never felt anything like this before.

Three words don't have enough meaning for what is felt

and so she whispered, I love you.

Beat of our Hearts

Resting my head against your chest

the music of your beating heart

Your presence is intoxicating

My fear no longer consuming me

I don't hide with you

It terrifies me how simple and easy it is to love you

So natural to me, easier then breathing,

I don't expect you to understand

I couldn't live another day not loving you

You, my love are divine,

you complete me, and yet I am wholly myself.

Trauma War

It hurt to open the wounds

The unsaid words between sisters

The words unspoken, now out

Like pandoras box

Theres no escaping these wounds

The bitter memories tainting their futures

Binding them stronger then blood

Understanding each other on another level

Day by day, they struggle, licking each others wounds

Showing a love that others may not understand

So they armour up ready to conquer

Another war they never should have known.

Secrets unshared

He didn't just hear her words

He heard everything she didn't say

The secrets unshared

He made it known to her

Yet, she still felt safe.

I love you

I love you

Everyday my love for you grows

The way you look deep in to my soul

Every touch sent tingles through my whole

To feel a love vibrate through my soul

It consumes my every being.

Time

Time is a cruel reality

Never having enough time

Not knowing when your time is up

Wishing to go back in time.

Moments missed, feeling robbed.

Fear

Its controlled my whole life

Being in fearful situations I find comfort knowing I can handle this evil

What if the next evil is too much, more evil

What if its the one that breaks me beyond repair

Change and all things new bring that fear back

New people, surroundings, what evil is going to be lurking in the sunlight

Give me darkness and wet any day, its harder for them to mask themselves then,

The true monsters are those perfectly made up ones

That's what scares me the most, loving another monster

Giving myself and my all to someone who doesn't deserve the goodness of my soul

Here I know exactly where my demons lie

I know how they intend on hurting me and I can take it, I
can handle it

When will I stop being scared, I know where my fear is
eased but it's not fair

How can I let someone be my safe haven

How can I put that burden on someone I love more then
I've loved before

It terrifies me, the fear freezes me.

You

I hope it's our story

I hope it's you I'm whispering during the moonlight

I hope its you featuring in my funniest stories

I hope it's your hand I'm holding in all the heartfelt moments

I hope it's you I find myself losing in those eyes

I hope it's your touch that I crave

I hope it's your smile I find with every entrance

I hope it's our love story, our children and grandchildren aspire for

Because it's you I hope for every minute of every day

Moonlight

Some people say your a ray of sunshine

I think that's for the faint hearted

Anyone can brighten a day that's bright

It takes someone special to lighten the darkness

Like the moonlight.

Be someone's moonlight

That's where the real magic is.

Old You

Don't waste your time missing the old you

There's a reason you are not that you anymore

Let her go

Grow and evolve to the person you were always meant to be

Run free, chase those dreams, don't go down without a fight,

your so much more than the old you because

the old you would be proud of the new you!

Farewell

To say goodbye to one you love

The pain of looking back, fond memories

Knowing you're not good for each other

Still having love there, not knowing what to do with that love

To continue to be hurt and hurt

It just can't be

So I listened to all the times I was told I was the problem

I listened to my own heart and how much it ached

To no longer be heard or want to hear

To love you was to hurt you

To be loved by you was hurting me.

So i farewell you, my sweet.

Weak

I read somewhere about weak emotions

It bothered me

How can feeling something be weak

I believe to feel is to be one of strength

You need to face your emotions, feel them, accept them

To truly show strength

To be able to sit with your emotions

Nothing weak about a person willing to accept their pain

The overwhelming feelings

To ignore those feelings is to be weak.

Desire

I never desired that fairytale life

I knew too much of the demons that haunted my waking hours

I was a being of pure positivity, I could see the rainbow in any storm

I knew how to dance before the pain, through the pain, let it pour,

When I was faced with a fairytale, I didn't know what to do

Do i run, is it a trick, it's too good to be true

I never wished for this in my life, it just wasn't possible

Everything happens for a reason, i constantly reminded myself

Where did this prince charming come from

Whisking Cinderella from the ball, from it all

Hiding in the meadows is where you will find them

Drinking in each other, their presence intoxicating.

To desire him, was a fear alone.

Too good to be true.

Familiarity

25

Their little faces, with eyes so bright

I could get lost in them, staring unknowingly

So familiar, it hurt

Wanting to hold them and never let go

I know baby, I know it hurts

It will be over soon

How? What do I do?

I can't fail them

Their little hopes and big dreams

Making wishes come true

Oh, the familiarity

Knowing you can't do it alone

Hoping they know they need to fight

I will be here, I will catch you

I'm not going anywhere

You have my heart

Oh, the familiarity

Where to go from here

Who to trust?

Come or Go

Oh, the familiarity

www.ingramcontent.com/pod-product-compliance
Lightning Source LLC
LaVergne TN
LVHW021348200726

843509LV00014B/2728